Letts

gets you through

PHONICS
SUCCESS
WORKBOOK

Ages 4–5

PHONICS

WORKBOOK

LOUIS FIDGE AND CHRISTINE MOORCROFT

Contents

Contents

Introduction

Phonics in the Foundation Stage (Ages 3 to 5)

Phonics is the relationship between sounds (phonemes) and letters or groups of letters (graphemes). Learning phonics involves listening to sounds, recognising sounds and discriminating between sounds as well as learning how sounds are represented by letters.

When first learning phonics, children should have many opportunities to enjoy listening to and reading stories, poems, songs and rhymes, as well as information books about topics that interest them.

How this book is organised

Letters of the alphabet (p. 6–13) introduces upper- and lower-case letters, in order, by name. You could use these terms with your child or 'capital letters' and 'lower-case letters' (as there is no other simple term for 'lower-case'). The letters are introduced in a way that helps children learn letter formation as well as position in the alphabet.

There are further activities on the letters of the alphabet at later stages of the book (p. 28–29, 58–59).

Initial letters of words introduces the sounds the letters represent in very short words in a similar order to that used in most schools. The most common sound is introduced for each letter. Most children notice the first sound of a word more easily than the others. Alternative sounds for each letter come later.

Middle sounds focuses on the middle vowel sound (a, e, i, o, u) of three-letter words that begin and end with a consonant. The activities use the most common sound for each vowel, i.e. the short vowel sounds 'a' as in cat, 'e' as in get, 'i' as in pin, 'o' as in hot and 'u' as in cup. Alternative sounds for these letters come later.

Two consonants – one sound introduces pairs of consonants that together stand for a single sound: 'ck' as in sock, 'ff' as in cuff, 'll' as in tell, 'ch' as in chop, 'sh' as in ship or fish, 'th' as in the, moth, path and with, and 'ng' at the end of words like sing. (Note that ng is not separated into n-g.) Other ch sounds come later. It is helpful to use the term 'two letters one sound' with children, so that they know that they should sound the two letters as one, rather than separately.

Consonant beginnings and endings introduces the more difficult and less commonly used consonants, some of which do not occur at the beginning of words: j, v, w, x, y, z. It also introduces zz and qu, since zz is more common than z at the ends of words and q is not used alone in English words.

Two vowels – one sound introduces some vowel sounds that are represented by two letters: ee, ai, oo, oa, ar, or, ur, ow, oi, er. Only one vowel sound (the simplest or most common) is used for each. Other vowel sounds for these pairs of letters come later, as do other ways of spelling the same vowel sounds.

Three vowels – one sound introduces vowel sounds represented by three letters: ear, ure, igh. Only one vowel sound (the simplest or most common) is used for each. Other vowel sounds for these sets of letters come later, as do other ways of spelling the same vowel sounds.

Consonant blends are groups of consonants that are sounded separately in a word and then blended to spell or say the word. The consonant s is used in this way in many words: for example, st, sn, sw, sk, sp, sn, sl. Other blended consonants introduced here are bl, fl, pl, cl, pr, br, tr, gr dr, cr, and, at the ends of words lt, lk, lm, lb, lf, lk, lp, nd, nt, nk.

What have I learned?

This section provides activities to help you and your child assess what has been learned. There are no pictures to use as clues – your child will use phonic knowledge only to read the words.

What the words mean

blend	Where two or more letters are sounded individually and then blended to read or spell a word.
consonant	The letters of the alphabet that are not **vowels**. Y can be used as either a vowel or a consonant. In English, **consonant phonemes** can be represented by more than one letter, for example: ch, th, sh, ng.
grapheme	The letter(s) that represents a **phoneme**. For example, the following graphemes can all represent the same phoneme: i (ibex, silent), y (cry, deny), igh (high, night), ie (cries, tried), i–e (bite, rice).
phoneme	The smallest unit of sound in a word. For example, 'cat' has three phonemes, represented by the letters c, a and t. A phoneme can be represented by two or more letters: f**or**t, h**igh**, n**eigh**.
vowel	The letters a, e, i, o and u. Y can also be used as a vowel, e.g. gym, rely. In English, some vowel **phonemes** are represented by groups of letters: or, ar, oo, igh, eigh.

Regional pronunciation will affect how your child pronounces some words. For example, the 'u' sound (as in 'cup', 'but' and 'sun') is often pronounced differently in different regions. This regional difference is not wrong.

ACKNOWLEDGEMENTS

The author and publisher are grateful to the copyright holders for permission to use quoted materials and images.

p.32 ©2009 Jupiterimages Corporation; p.65 ©iStockphoto/Thinkstock, ©Hemera/Thinkstock; p.67 ©iStockphoto/Thinkstock; p.70 ©iStockphoto/Thinkstock; p.72 ©Hemera/Thinkstock; p.73 ©iStockphoto/Thinkstock; p.74 ©iStockphoto/Thinkstock; p.76 ©Clipart.com; p.78 ©liquidlibrary/Thinkstock; p.90 ©iStockphoto/Thinkstock; all other images ©Shutterstock.com

Every effort has been made to trace copyright holders and obtain their permission for the use of copyright material. The author and publisher will gladly receive information enabling them to rectify any error or omission in subsequent editions. All facts are correct at time of going to press.

Published by Letts Educational
An imprint of HarperCollinsPublishers Ltd
1 London Bridge Street
London SE1 9GF

ISBN 9780008294229

First published 2013

This edition published 2018

1 0 9 8 7 6 5 4 3

© Letts Educational, an imprint of HarperCollinsPublishers Limited 2018

Text © Louis Fidge and HarperCollinsPublishers Ltd

Commissioning editor: Tammy Poggo
Authors: Louis Fidge and Christine Moorcroft
Project editor: Charlotte Christensen
Cover design: Paul Oates
Inside concept design: Letts Educational
Text design and layout: Planman Technologies
Artwork: Nigel Kitching, Geoff Ward and Planman Technologies
Production: Natalia Rebow
Printed and bound in Great Britain by Martins the Printers

The alphabet a-d

Letters a-d

Write the letters.

Say the names of the letters.

Colour them on the alphabet ladder.

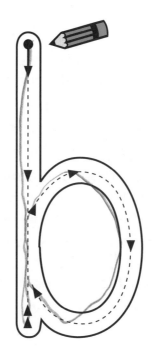

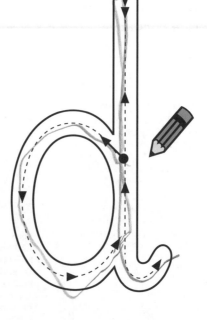

A	a
B	b
C	c
D	d
E	e
F	f
G	g
H	h
I	i
J	j
K	k
L	l
M	m
N	n
O	o
P	p
Q	q
R	r
S	s
T	t
U	u
V	v
W	w
X	x
Y	y
Z	z

Letters e–i

Write the letters.

Say the names of the letters.

Colour them on the alphabet ladder.

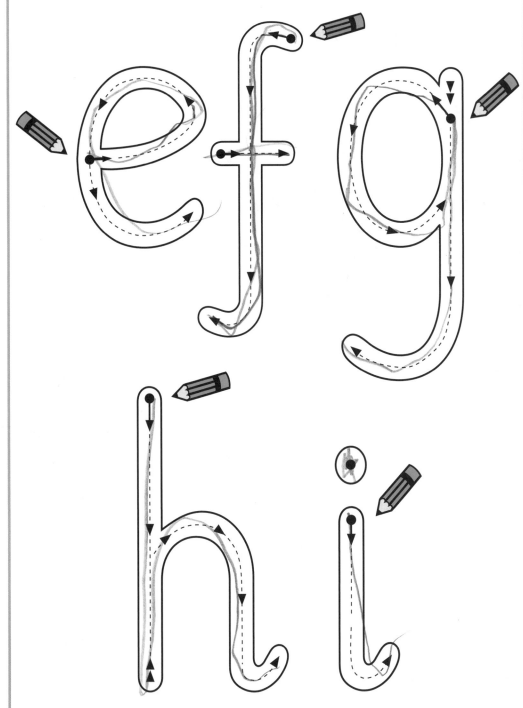

A a
B b
C c
D d
E e
F f
G g
H h
I i
J j
K k
L l
M m
N n
O o
P p
Q q
R r
S s
T t
U u
V v
W w
X x
Y y
Z z

The alphabet j–n

Letters j–n

Write the letters.

Say the names of the letters.

Colour them on the alphabet ladder.

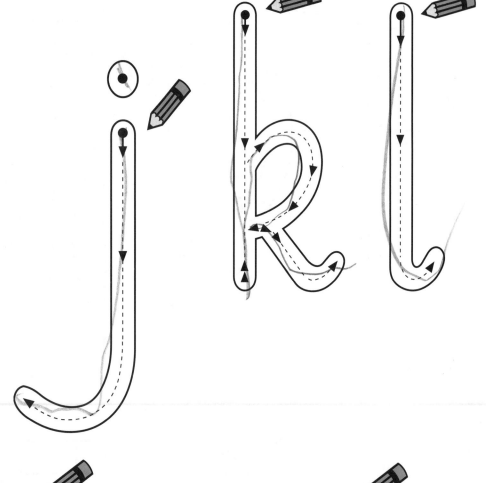

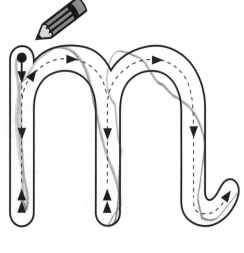

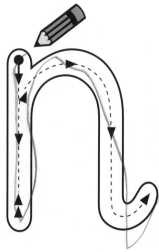

A	a
B	b
C	c
D	d
E	e
F	f
G	g
H	h
I	i
J	j
K	k
L	l
M	m
N	n
O	o
P	p
Q	q
R	r
S	s
T	t
U	u
V	v
W	w
X	x
Y	y
Z	z

Letters o–r

Write the letters.

Say the names of the letters.

Colour them on the alphabet ladder.

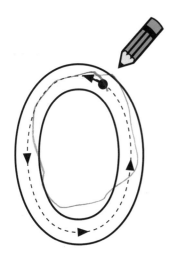

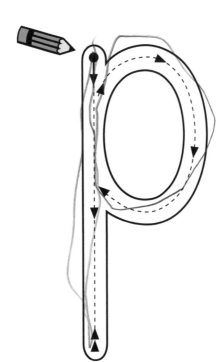

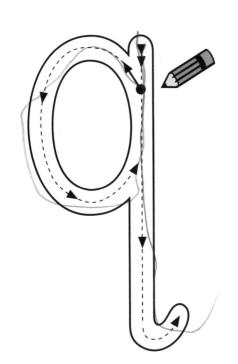

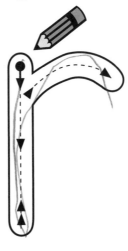

A a
B b
C c
D d
E e
F f
G g
H h
I i
J j
K k
L l
M m
N n
O o
P p
Q q
R r
S s
T t
U u
V v
W w
X x
Y y
Z z

The alphabet s–v

Letters s–v

Write the letters.

Say the names of the letters.

Colour them on the alphabet ladder.

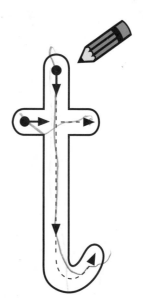
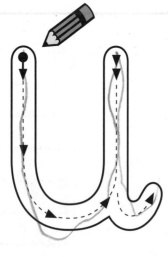

| A a |
| B b |
| C c |
| D d |
| E e |
| F f |
| G g |
| H h |
| I i |
| J j |
| K k |
| L l |
| M m |
| N n |
| O o |
| P p |
| Q q |
| R r |
| S s |
| T t |
| U u |
| V v |
| W w |
| X x |
| Y y |
| Z z |

Letters w-z

Write the letters.

Say the names of the letters.

Colour them on the alphabet ladder.

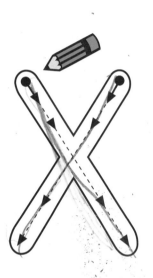
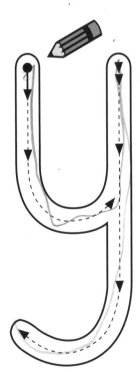
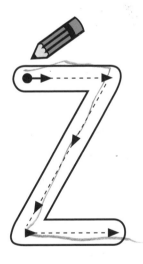

A a
B b
C c
D d
E e
F f
G g
H h
I i
J j
K k
L l
M m
N n
O o
P p
Q q
R r
S s
T t
U u
V v
W w
X x
Y y
Z z

Upper- and lower-case letter matching

Matching letters a–m

Match each rocket to its planet.

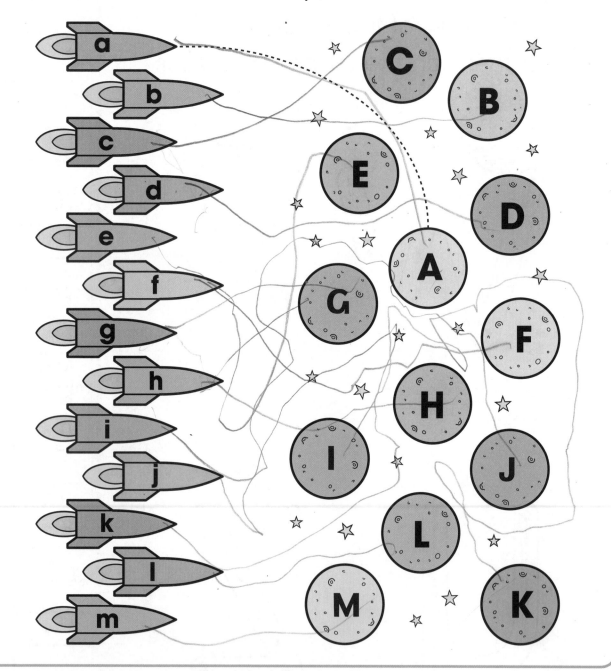

Parent's tip Use the names of the letters, not the sounds they represent. If your child still has difficulty recognising the letters, provide plasticine or modelling clay and help him/her to make some upper- and lower-case letters to match (beginning with the first four).

Upper- and lower-case letter matching

Matching letters n–z

Park each van in its correct place.

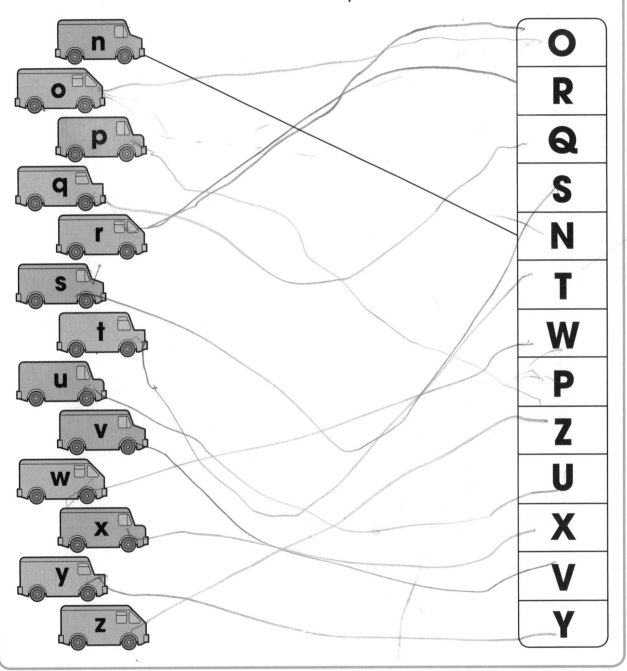

Letters and sounds s, t, p, n

Letters and sounds

What's in the box?
Say the words.
Write the first letter
of each word.

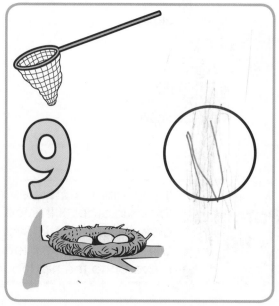

Letters and sounds

What's in the box?
Say the words.
Write the first letter
of each word.

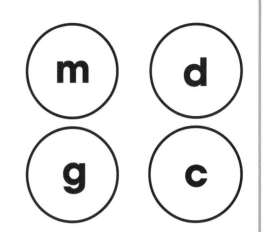

Letters and sounds k, r, h, b

Letters and sounds

What's in the box?
Say the words.
Write the first letter
of each word.

(k) (r)

(h) (b)

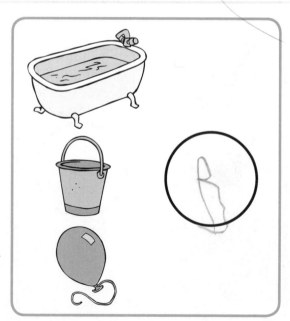

Letters and sounds

What's in the box?
Say the words.
Write the first letter
of each word.

(l) (f)

(a) (e)

a in the middle

Read the rhyme

a m**a**n in a v**a**n with a f**a**n

a words

Say the words.

Write the letters for the sounds. Write the words.

m	a	n

m a n

Write another rhyming word.

	a	n

Rhyming words

Say some words that rhyme with **cat**.
Write the letters for the sounds. Write the words.

| c | a | t |

cat

| | | |

| | | |

Make up a rhyme about a cat. Draw a picture.

e in the middle

Read the rhyme

ten men and a hen

e words

Say the words.

Write the letters for the sounds. Write the words.

| m | e | n |

10

| | | |

| | | |

Write another rhyming word.

| | e | n |

Rhyming words

Say some words that rhyme with **wet**.
Write the letters for the sounds. Write the words.

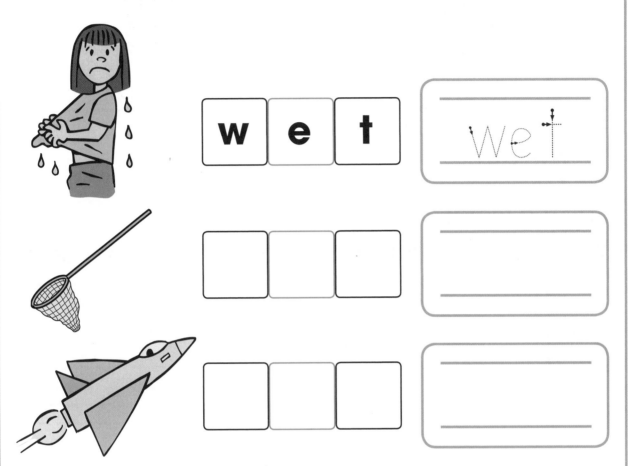

w	e	t

wet

Make up a rhyme about a jet. Draw a picture.

i in the middle

Read the rhymes

a p**i**n in a t**i**n

a t**i**n in a b**i**n

i words

Say the words.

Write the letters for the sounds. Write the words.

| t | i | n |

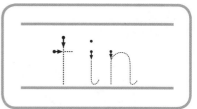

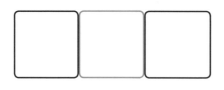

Write another rhyming word.

Rhyming words

Say some words that rhyme with **big**.

Write the letters for the sounds. Write the words.

b	i	g

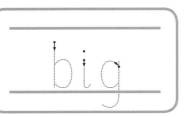
big

Make up a rhyme about something big.

Draw a picture.

o in the middle

Read the rhyme

a d**o**g on a l**o**g in a f**o**g

o words

Say the words.

Write the letters for the sounds. Write the words.

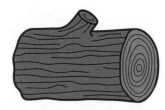  

 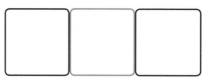 

Write another rhyming word.

Rhyming words

Say some words that rhyme with **hop**.
Write the letters for the sounds. Write the words.

h	o	p

hop

Make up a rhyme about something that goes pop. Draw a picture.

u in the middle

Read the rhymes

a b**u**g in a m**u**g

a b**u**g in a j**u**g

u words

Say the words.

Write the letters for the sounds. Write the words.

| b | u | g |

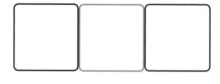

Write another rhyming word.

| | u | g |

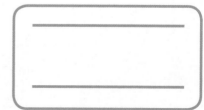

Rhyming words

Say some words that rhyme with **rub**.
Write the letters for the sounds. Write the words.

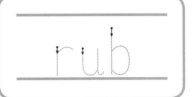

r	u	b

rub

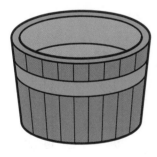

Make up a rhyme about a cub. Draw a picture.

27

The alphabet

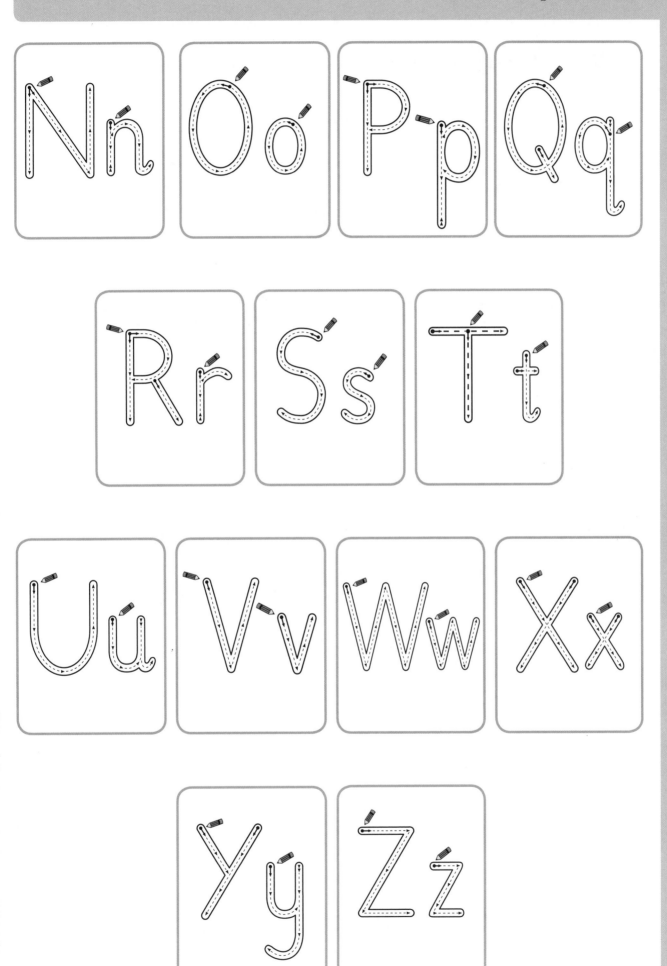

Words ending –ck

Read the words

Read the words. Write the words.

s → a → ck   s → o → ck   s → u → ck

_____   _____   _____

Make the words

Make some other words. Read the words.
Write the words.

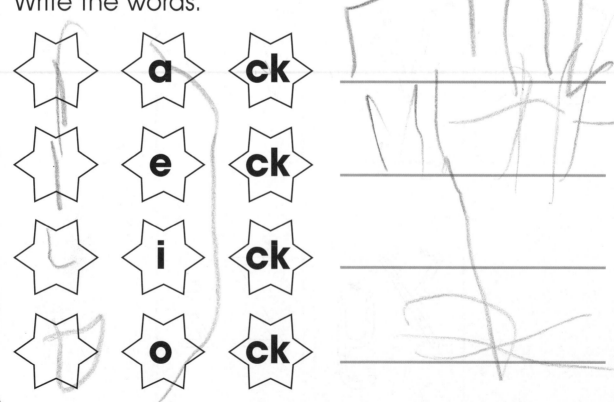

☆   a   ck   _____

☆   e   ck   _____

☆   i   ck   _____

☆   o   ck   _____

Read the words

Read the words. Write the words.

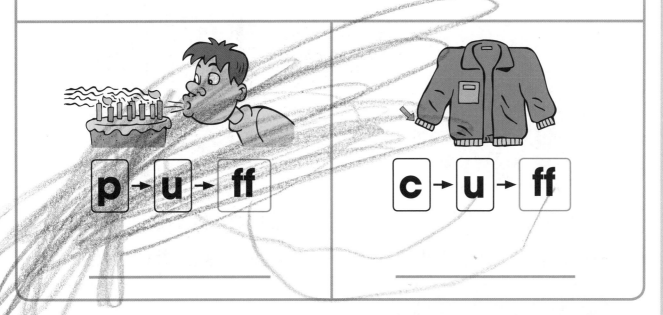

p → u → ff

c → u → ff

_____   _____

Read the rhyme

Huff and puff
Danny Duff

Write the words

Write some words that end **ff**.
Use these letters:

o m u

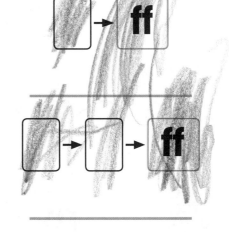

→ **ff**

_____

→ → **ff**

_____

Read the words.

Words ending -ll

Read the rhymes

Circle **ll** in the rhymes.

Jack and Jill
went up the hill.

Ding, dong, dell,
Pussy's in the well.

Make the words

Make the words. Read the words. Write the words.

| □ | → | □ | → | **ll** | _____ |

| **p** | → | □ | → | **ll** | _____ |

| **y** | → | □ | → | □ | _____ |

| **m** | → | □ | → | □ | _____ |

Read the words

Read the words. Write the words.

_____   _____

Read the rhyme

Hug and ki**ss**
Little Mi**ss** Bli**ss**

Write the words

Write some words
that end **ss**.
Use these letters:
o b l e

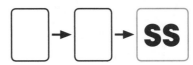

_____

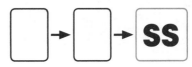

Read the words.

Words beginning ch-

Say the word.
Hear the sound.

chop

Write the letters.

Circle the ch- words

Circle the things that start **ch**. Say the words.

Parent's tip   You could play a game in which you make up (but do not write) sentences with 'ch'. For example: Chuck the chimp chooses cheese, Charlie chased a chicken, Cheryl chooses cherries.

Words beginning ch-

Make the words

Make some words. Read the words. Write the words.

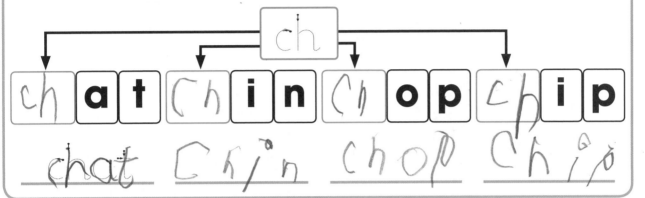

chat   Chin   chop   Chip

Choose the words

Choose the correct word for each picture.
Write the word.

 chat or chin?

 chop or chip?

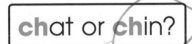

_____   _____

Make the words

Make some more words. Read the words. Write the
words.

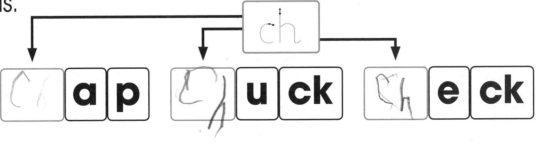

_____   _____   _____

Words beginning sh-

Say the word.
Hear the sound.

ship

Write the letters.

Circle the sh- words

Circle the things that start **sh**. Say the words.

Parent's tip

You could play a game in which you take turns to say what is in the sheep's shed. All words must begin with 'sh'. For example: in the sheep's shed is a ship, in the sheep's shed is a shoe….a shell... a sheet (and so on). To make it harder, try to repeat everything that has already been said.

Read the words

Read the words. Write the words.

sh → i → p	sh → o → p	sh → e → d
ship		

Write the words

Write the word for each picture.

_____   _____   _____

Make the words

Make some more words that start **sh**.

Read the words. Write the words.

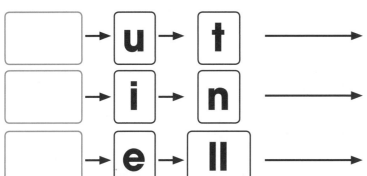

☐ → u → t → ⟶ _____

☐ → i → n → ⟶ _____

☐ → e → ll → ⟶ _____

Words ending –sh

Read the words

Read the words. Write the words.

m → a → sh	h → u → sh	d → i → sh
m a s h		

Write the words

Write the word for each picture.

 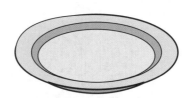 

——— ——— ———

Make the words

Make some more words that end **sh**.
Read the words. Write the words.

w → i → ☐ → ⟶ ————

b → a → ☐ → ⟶ ————

p → o → ☐ → ⟶ ————

Make the words

Add **sh** to complete each word.
Read the words.

ca _____

di_____

_____ip

ma _____

_____ell

fi _____

Write the words that begin **sh** in me.

Write the words that end **sh** in me.

Words with th

Say the word.
Hear the sound.

ba**th**

Write the letters.

Read the sentence

Circle **th** in the sentence.

This is Beth the moth on the path.

Parent's tip

This activity features letters and sounds your child has learned from previous pages. You could also encourage him/her to notice everyday words that begin or end with 'th'. Say the words, emphasising the 'th' sound. For example: Thursday, cloth, this, that, those, these, thing, thinking.

Make the words

Add **th** to complete each word. Read the words.

 _____ **in**

 _____ **ick**

 **ba** _____

 **mo** _____

 **pa** _____

Make the words

Make some more words with **th**.

Read the words. Write the words.

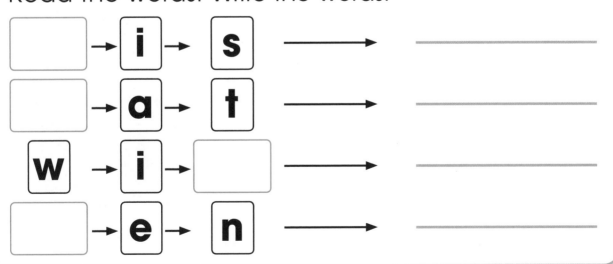

	→ **i** → **s**	→	_____
	→ **a** → **t**	→	_____
w → **i** →		→	_____
	→ **e** → **n**	→	_____

Words ending –ng

Read the words

Read the words. Write the words

r → i → ng	k → i → ng	s → i → ng
_____	_____	_____

Read the rhyme

Circle **ng** in the rhyme.

Ding! Dong! Ding!
Ring, bells, ring.

Dong! Ding! Dong!
Sing a song.

Make the words

Add **ng** to complete each word.

Read the words.

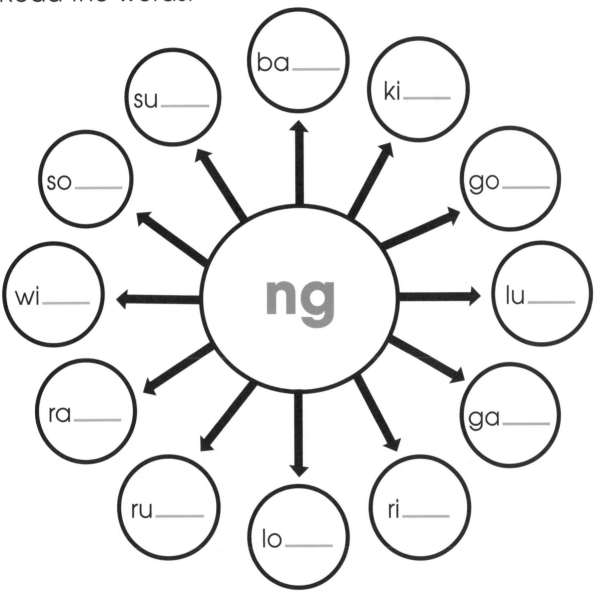

ba____

su____

ki____

so____

go____

wi____

ng

lu____

ra____

ga____

ru____

lo____

ri____

Parent's tip

The letters 'ng' represent a single sound and should not be 'sounded' separately. You could practise the sound with your child by making up silly songs (like the ones on p. 42). You could make up some 'ng' words, too!, For example:

Sing a song, it won't be long

Jango, Jango, do the tango

Ring bell ring; Ring for the king.

Letter j

Say the word.
Hear the sound.

jam

Write the letter.

Circle the j words

Circle the things that start j. Say the words.

Words starting j

Colour **j** on the ladder.

Say the words for the pictures.

Circle the things that start **j**.

A a
B b
C c
D d
E e
F f
G g
H h
I i
J j
K k
L l
M m
N n
O o
P p
Q q
R r
S s
T t
U u
V v
W w
X x
Y y
Z z

Letter v

Say the word.
Hear the sound.

van

Write the letter.

Circle the v words

Circle the things that start **v**. Say the words.

Words starting v

Colour **v** on the ladder.

Say the words for the pictures.

Circle the things that start **v**.

A a
B b
C c
D d
E e
F f
G g
H h
I i
J j
K k
L l
M m
N n
O o
P p
Q q
R r
S s
T t
U u
V v
W w
X x
Y y
Z z

Letter w

Say the word.
Hear the sound.

web

Write the letter.

Circle the w words

Circle the things that start **w**. Say the words.

Words starting w

Colour **w** on the ladder.

Say the words for the pictures.

Circle the things that start **w**.

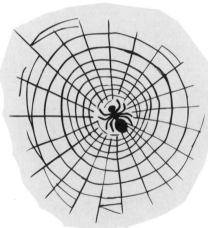

A a
B b
C c
D d
E e
F f
G g
H h
I i
J j
K k
L l
M m
N n
O o
P p
Q q
R r
S s
T t
U u
V v
W w
X x
Y y
Z z

Letter x

Say the word.
Hear the sound.

bo**x**

Write the letter.

Circle the x words

Circle the things with **x** in them. Say the words.

Words with the letter x

Colour **x** on the ladder.

Say the words for the pictures.
Circle the things with **x** in them.

Letter y

Say the word.
Hear the sound.

yak

Write the letter.

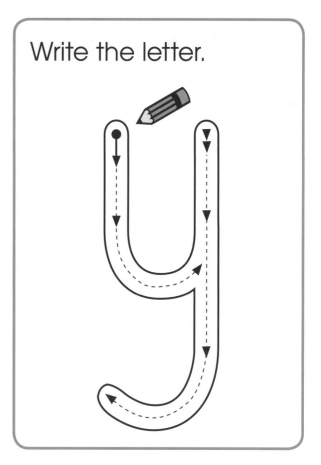

Circle the y words

Circle the things that start with **y**. Say the words.

Words starting y

Colour **y** on the ladder.

Circle the things that start **y**.

Say the words for the pictures.

| A a |
| B b |
| C c |
| D d |
| E e |
| F f |
| G g |
| H h |
| I i |
| J j |
| K k |
| L l |
| M m |
| N n |
| O o |
| P p |
| Q q |
| R r |
| S s |
| T t |
| U u |
| V v |
| W w |
| X x |
| Y y |
| Z z |

Words beginning z

Say the word.
Hear the sound.

zip

Write the letter.

Circle the z words

Circle the things that start **z**. Say the words.

Make the words

Make some words that start **z**.
Read the words. Write the words.

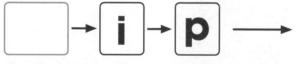

→ **i** → **p** → _____

→ **a** → **p** → _____

→ **e** → **d** → _____

Words ending zz

Make words that end **zz**.

Read the words.

bu_____

fi_____

ja_____

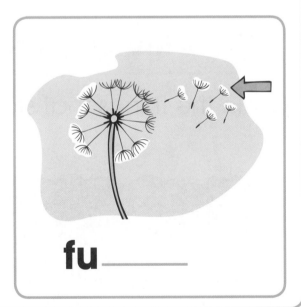

fu_____

Parent's tip

Before starting this page, practise the 'zz' sound with your child by saying 'buzz' with an emphasis on the 'zz'. You could use 'zz' words in 'silly' questions. For example: Do bees fizz? No, bees buzz; Do bees play jazz? No, bees just buzz; Do bees have fuzz? Yes, bees have fuzz, and they buzz.

Words beginning qu

Say the word.
Hear the sound.

queen

Write the letters.

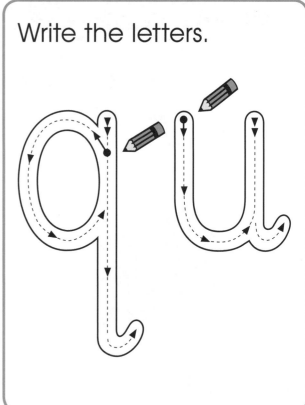

Circle the qu words

Circle the things that start **qu**. Say the words.

Qu words

Say the words for the pictures.
Circle the things that start **qu**.

Make the words

Make some words that start **qu**.
Read the words. Write the words.

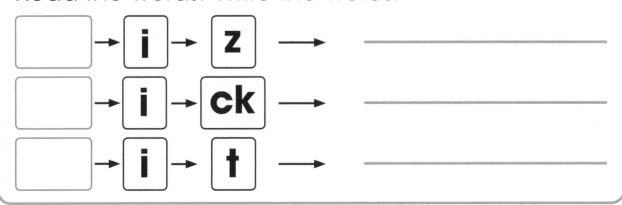

	i	z	→	_____
	i	ck	→	_____
	i	t	→	_____

Alphabetical order

Activity 1

Join the letters to take the frog across the river.

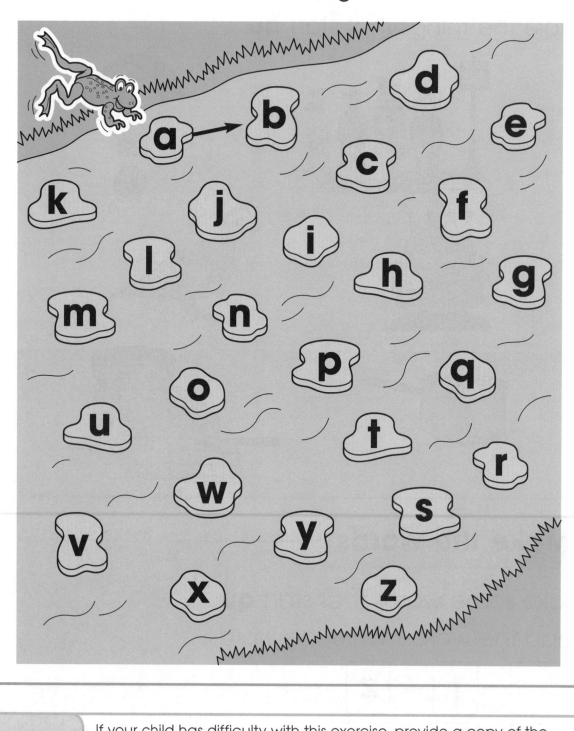

Parent's tip

If your child has difficulty with this exercise, provide a copy of the alphabet in lower-case letters so that he/she can check what comes next after 'landing' on each letter. After completing the page you could ask him/her to follow the frog's route and say the names of the letters. Children who find this easy might enjoy saying them in reverse order, or finding the letters before and after given letters. For example, 'Which letter comes after j?', 'Which letter comes before p?'

Activity 2

Join the letters to draw an animal.
Colour the animal.

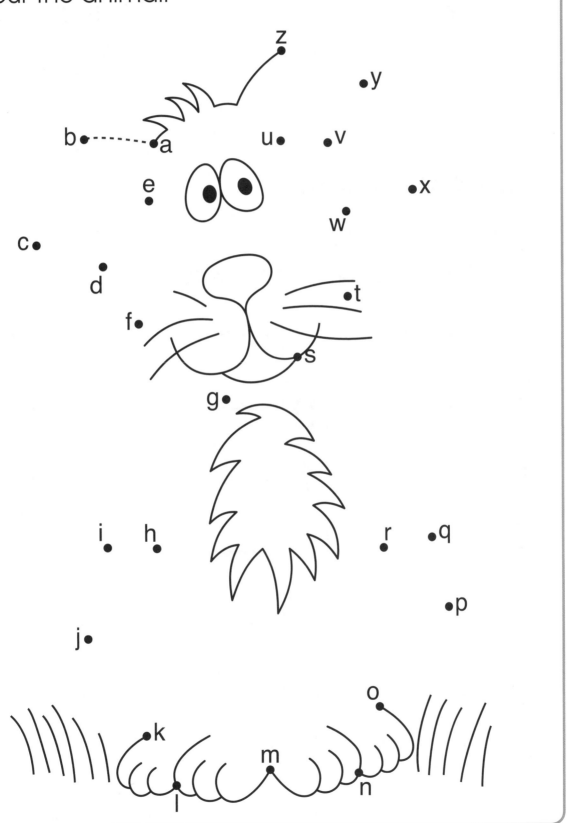

Words with ee

sh → ee → p

sheep

Write the letters.

Make the words

Make the **ee** words.

Read the words. Write the words.

☐ → **l** → _____

k → ☐ → **p** → _____

b → ☐ → **f** → _____

s → ☐ → **k** → _____

f → ☐ → **l** → _____

n → ☐ → **d** → _____

ch → ☐ → **k** → _____

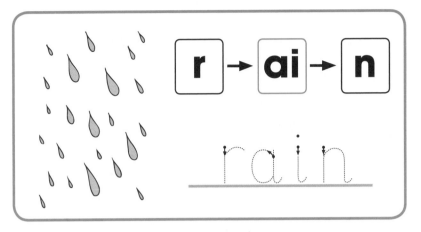

r → ai → n

rain

Circle the ai words

Circle the things with **ai**.
Say the words.

Make the words

Make some **ai** words.
Read the words. Write the words.

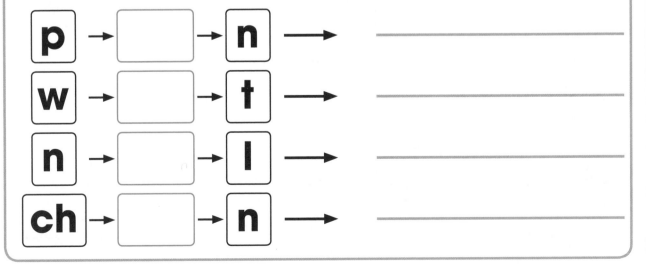

p → ☐ → n → _____

w → ☐ → t → _____

n → ☐ → l → _____

ch → ☐ → n → _____

Words with oo

m → oo → n

moon

Write the letters.

Make the words

Make the **oo** words.

Read the words. Write the words.

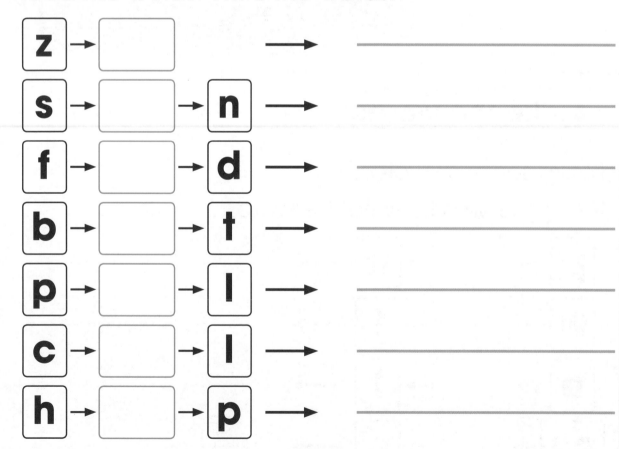

z → ☐ → _____

s → ☐ → n → _____

f → ☐ → d → _____

b → ☐ → t → _____

p → ☐ → l → _____

c → ☐ → l → _____

h → ☐ → p → _____

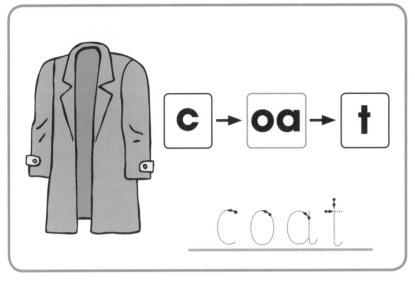

c → oa → t

coat

Write the letters.

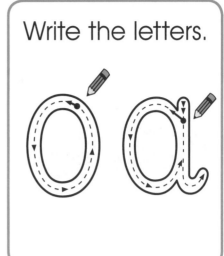

Make the words

Make the **oa** words.

Read the words. Write the words.

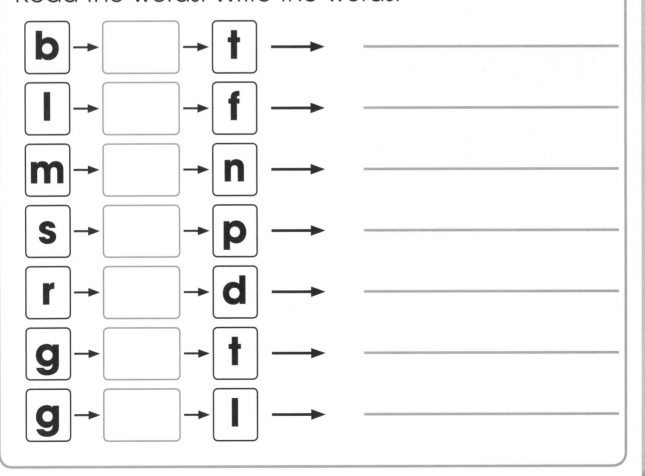

b → ☐ → t → _____

l → ☐ → f → _____

m → ☐ → n → _____

s → ☐ → p → _____

r → ☐ → d → _____

g → ☐ → t → _____

g → ☐ → l → _____

Words with ar

c → **ar**

car

Write the letters.

Make the words

The dogs b [ ] k

in the p [ ] k.

The dogs b [ ] k at the

c [ ] in the d [ ] k.

Make the **ar** words.

Read the words. Write the words.

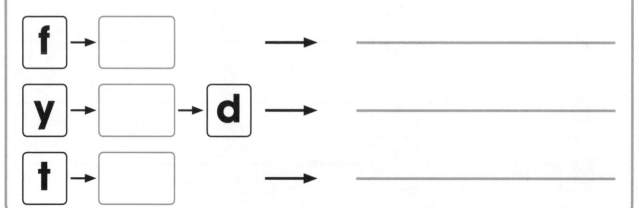

f → [ ] → _____

y → [ ] → **d** → _____

t → [ ] → _____

Make the words

Add **ar** to complete the words. Read the words.

d____**t**

f____**m**

____**k**

____**m**

c____**d**

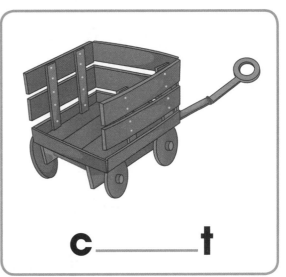

c____**t**

Words with or

t → **or** → **ch**

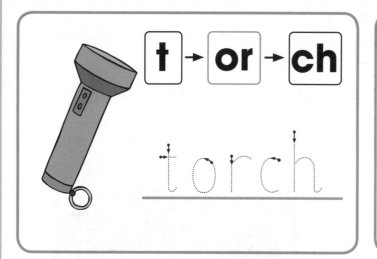

torch

Write the letters.

Circle the or words

Circle the things with **or**.
Say the words.

Make the words

Make the **or** words. Read the words. Write the words.

h	→		→	n	→	_____
c	→		→	n	→	_____
f	→		→	k	→	_____
s	→		→	t	→	_____

Make the words

Add **or** to complete the words. Read the words.

f___t

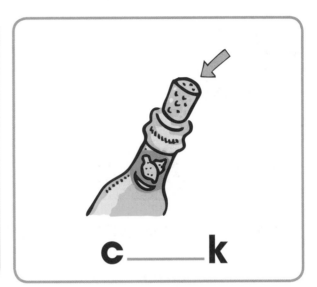

c___k

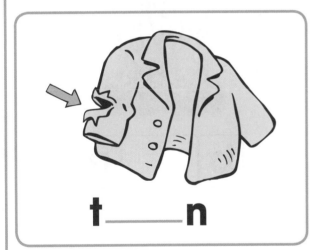

t___n

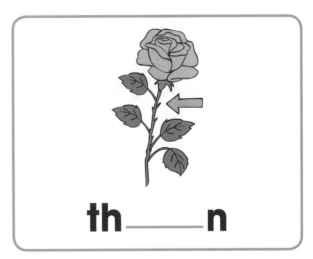

th___n

n___th

p___ch

Words with ur

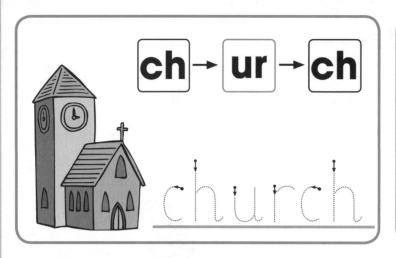

ch → ur → ch

church

Write the letters.

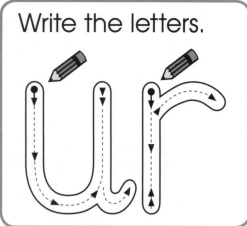

Make the words

Make the **ur** words. Read the words. Write the words.

| f | |

| b | | n |

| c | | l |

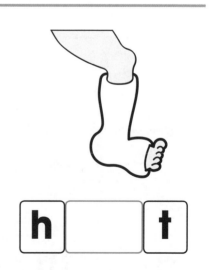

| h | | t |

Make the words

Make the words with **ur**. Read the words.
Write the words.

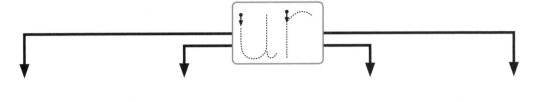

f___   b___n   t___n   h___t

_f_u_r_   _____   _____   _____

ch___n   ch___   ch___   s___f   t___f

_____   _____   _____   _____

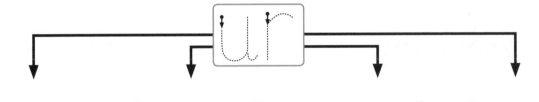

c___l T___kish   f___nish t___nip

_____   _____   _____   _____

Words with ow

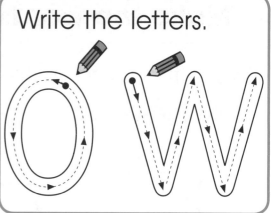

Write the letters.

Make the words

Make the **ow** words. Read the words. Write the words.

 l

 t n

b

g n

Words with ow

Read the words

Read the words. Write the words.

c → ow	d → ow → n	h → ow → l

Write the words

Write the word for each picture.

Make the words

Make some words with **ow**.
Read the words. Write the words.

n → ☐ → _____

h → ☐ → _____

w → ☐ → _____

Words with oi

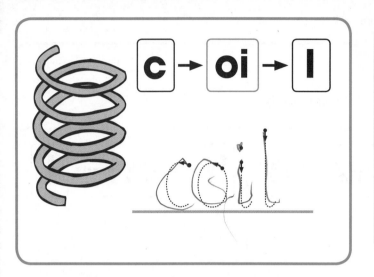

c → oi → l

coil

Write the letters.

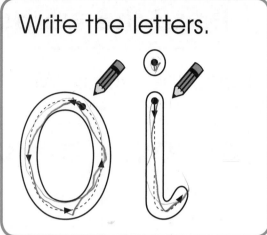

Make the words

Make the **oi** words. Read the words. Write the words.

o l

b o i l

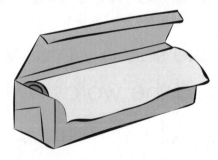

c o i n

f o i l

72

Read the words

Read the words. Write the words.

j → oi → n	s → oi → l	qu → oi → t
join	_sojl_	_quot_

Write the words

Write the word for each picture.

_____   _____   _____

Make the words

Make some words with **oi**.
Read the words. Write the words.

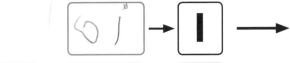

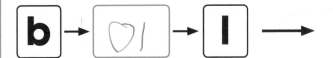

oi → l → _oil_

c → oi → l → _coil_

b → oi → l → _boil_

Words with er

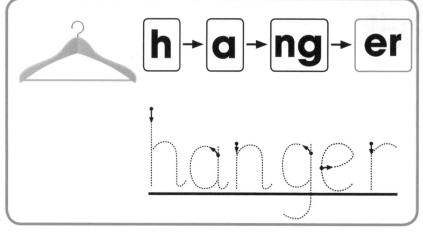

h → a → ng → er

hanger

Write the letters.

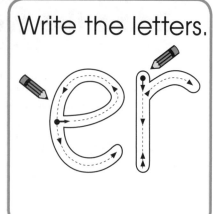

Make the words

Make the **er** words. Read the words. Write the words.

| b | oi | l | |

| r | o | ck | |

| p | ee | l | |

| f | ee | l | |

Words with er

Read the words

Read the words. Write the words.

b ▸ o ▸ x ▸ er	m ▸ a ▸ sh ▸ er	b ▸ u ▸ zz ▸ er
boxer	_____	_____

Write the words

Write the word for each picture.

_____   _____   _____

Make the words

Make some words with **er**.
Read the words. Write the words.

sh → ow → ☐	→ _____
b → a → ng → ☐	→ _____
s → u → ff → ☐	→ _____

Words with ear

h → **ear**

hear

Write the letters.

Make the words

Make the **ear** words.

Read the words. Write the words.

t →

f →

d →

g →

Make the words

Make some words with **ear**. Read the words.
Write the words.

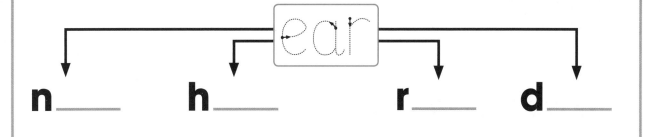

n_____   h_____   r_____   d_____

_____   _____   _____   _____

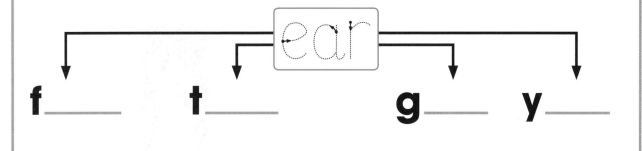

f_____   t_____   g_____   y_____

_____   _____   _____   _____

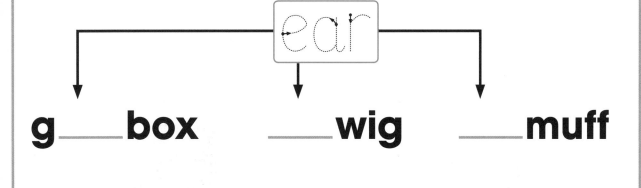

g_____**box**   _____**wig**   _____**muff**

_____   _____   _____

Parent's tip	Say some sentences and ask your child to spot the words with 'ear'. For example: Clear your ears so you'll hear the gears. The gears in the gearbox go clunk I fear. This year I'm nearly thirty. Oh dear, the rear of my ear is sore.

Words with air

ch → **air**

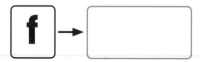

Write the letters.

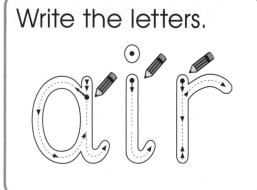

Make the words

Make the **air** words. Read the words.
Write the words.

f →

h →

p →

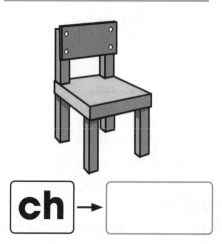

ch →

| c | → | **ure** |

Dr Dure and his cure.

Write the letters.

Make the words

Make **ure** words.

Read the words. Write the words.

p	→		→	——————
c	→		→	——————
s	→		→	——————

| **i** | → | **n** | → | **s** | → | | → | —————— |

| **m** | → | **a** | → | **n** | → | | → | —————— |

Words with igh

n → igh → t

night

Write the letters.

igh

Read the rhyme

Circle **igh** in the rhyme.

Good night, sleep tight.
Wake up in the morning light
To do what is right with all your might.

Read the words

Read the words. Write the words.

h → **igh**	r → **igh** → t	l → **igh** → t
high	_____	_____

n → **igh** → t	f → **igh** → t	t → **igh** → t
_____	_____	_____

Write the words

Write the correct word under each picture.

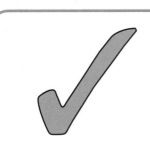

_____

_____

_____

_____

_____

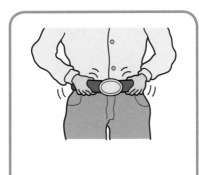

_____

Words with s + consonant t

Read the words

Read the words with **st**. Write the words.

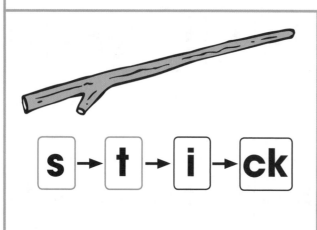

s → t → i → ck

_____

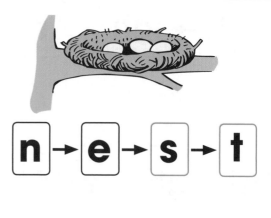

n → e → s → t

_____

Read the sentences

Circle the words with **st**.

I did my best in the test.

I ran fast but still came last!

Parent's tip

Ask your child to write words that rhyme with best: nest, west, test, chest, pest, rest, quest. Do the same for words that rhyme with fast: cast, last, mast, past, vast. Together, you could make up other rhyming sentences like the ones on this page.

Write the words

Make some words. Read the words.

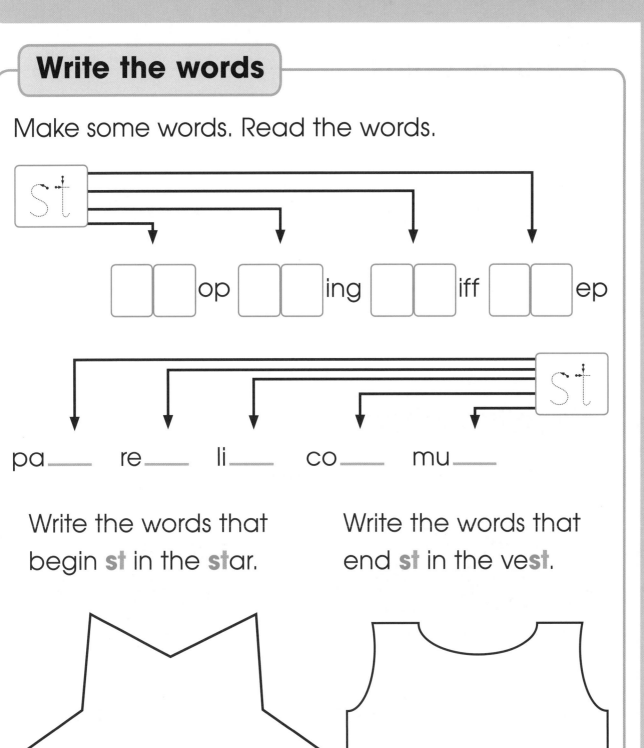

st

☐☐op ☐☐ing ☐☐iff ☐☐ep

pa___ re___ li___ co___ mu___

st

Write the words that
begin **st** in the **st**ar.

Write the words that
end **st** in the ve**st**.

Words beginning s + consonant

Read the words

Read the words. Write the words.

s → n → i → ff

s → w → i → ng

Write the letters

Write the missing letters. Read the words.

I can [ ] **w** **i** **m** .

I can [ ] **k** **i** **p** .

I can [ ] **p** **i** **n** .

I can [ ] **n** **i** **p** .

Read the words

Read the words. Write the words.

s → l → i → p

s → t → i → ck

s → p → e → ll

s → m → a → sh

_____   _____

Make the words

Make another word. Read the word. Write the word.

☐ → k → i → n → _____

Words beginning consonant + l

Read the words

Read the words. Write the words.

| b | → | l | → | a | → | ck |

_____

| b | → | l | → | o | → | t |

_____

| f | → | l | → | a | → | g | → | s |

_____

| f | → | l | → | a | → | p |

_____

| p | → | l | → | o | → | p |

_____

| c | → | l | → | o | → | p |

_____

Read the words

Read the words. Write the words.

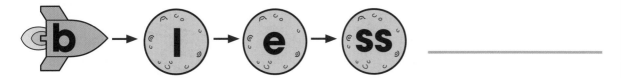

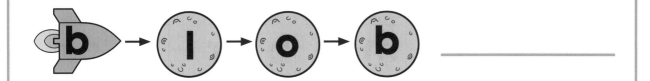

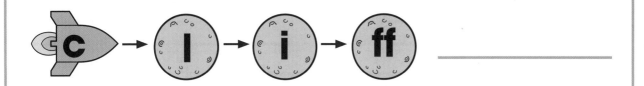

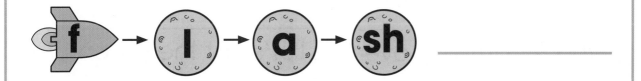

Make the words

Complete the words. Read the words.
Write the words.

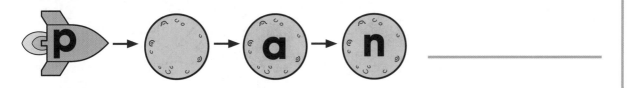

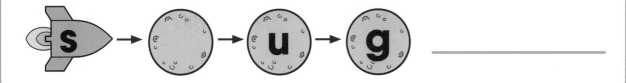

Words beginning consonant + r

Read the words

Read the words. Write the words.

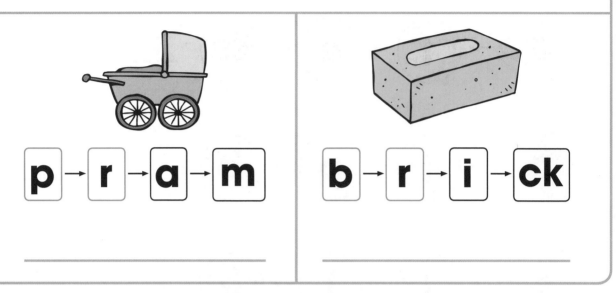

p → r → a → m

b → r → i → ck

Talk about the picture

Who is **tr**amping over my **br**idge?

Let's eat the **gr**een **gr**ass.

trip! **tr**ap! **tr**ip! **tr**ap!

the **tr**oll

the **thr**ee Billy Goats **Gr**uff

Read the words

Read the words. Write the words.

b → r → i → ng _____

b → r → i → ck _____

c → r → a → ck _____

c → r → a → sh _____

Make the words

Complete the words. Read the words.
Write the words.

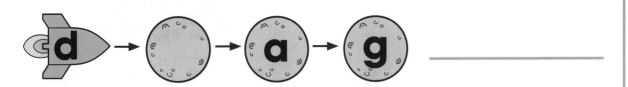

d → ○ → a → g _____

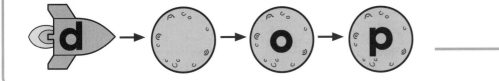

d → ○ → o → p _____

Words ending l + consonant

Read the words

Read the words. Write the words.

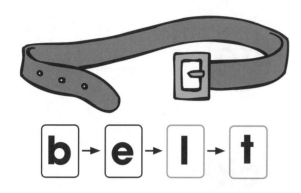

b → e → l → t

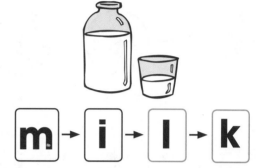

m → i → l → k

e → l → m

k → i → l → t

b → u → l → b

f → i → l → m

Make the words

Make the words. Read the words.

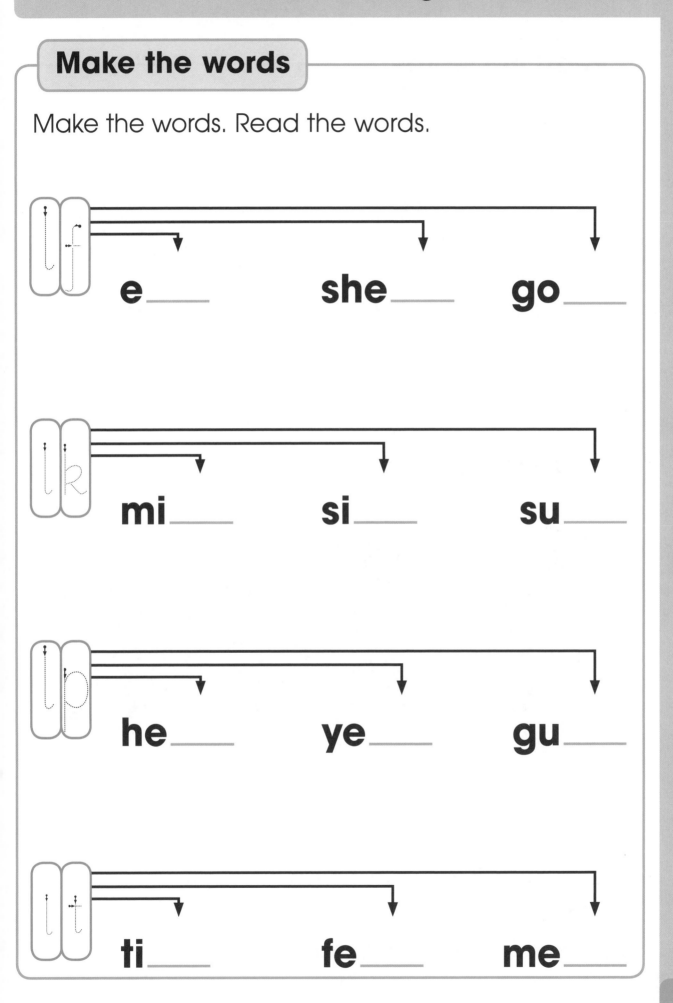

e___   she___   go___

mi___   si___   su___

he___   ye___   gu___

ti___   fe___   me___

Words ending n + consonant

Read the words

Read the words. Write the words.

p → o → n → d

_____

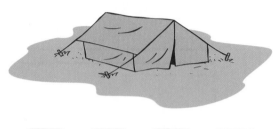

t → e → n → t

_____

Read the rhyme

The ba**nd** is on the sa**nd**.

The sa**nd** is on the la**nd**.

Wave a ha**nd** to the ba**nd** on the sa**nd** –

on the la**nd**.

Isn't that gra**nd**? – A ba**nd** on the sa**nd**.

Read the words

Read the words. Write the words.

| p | → | o | → | n | → | d |

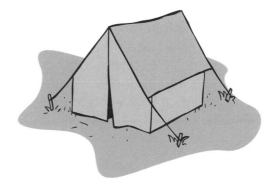

| t | → | e | → | n | → | t |

_____

| s | → | i | → | n | → | k |

| h | → | a | → | n | → | d |

_____

Make the words

Make another word. Read the word. Write the word.

| | → | u | → | n | → | k | ⟶ | _____ |

What have I learned?

Test 1

Say the word for each picture.
Write the letter it starts with.

Test 2

Say the word for each picture.
Write the letter it starts with.

Test 3

Read the words.

mat	ran
den	fig
pot	rug

Test 4

Read the words.

back	huff
fell	fuss
buzz	rag

Test 5

Read the words and names.

chess	shell
chip	bush
than	Beth

Test 6

Read the words and names.

fang	Jack
vet	web
fix	yap

What have I learned?

Test 7

Read the words.

quiz	peel
zoom	toad
hard	fork

Test 8

Read the words.

charm	turn
vow	join
farmer	fear

Test 9

Read the words.

hair	pure
light	staff
vest	spear

Test 10

Read the words.

quill	blend
slush	clang
orbit	shelter